ACT NOW!
Monologues for Young People
by M6 Theatre

A Friend Request
Kate Collins

Father's Footsteps
Mary Cooper

A Change for the Better
Anne Neville

Cheers
Ged McKenna

Web Pal & *It Should Have Been* Me
Billy Cowan

Published by Playdead Press 2014

© *A Friend Request* by Kate Collins
© *Father's Footsteps* by Mary Cooper
© *A Change for the Better* by Anne Neville
© *Cheers* by Ged McKenna
© *Web Pal & It Should Have Been Me* by Billy Cowan

Each writer has asserted their rights under the Copyright, Design and Patents Act, 1988, to be identified as the author of their work.

A CIP catalogue record for this book is available from the British Library.

ISBN 978-1-910067-11-6

Caution

All rights whatsoever in this play are strictly reserved and application for performance should be sought through the author before rehearsals begin. No performance may be given unless a license has been obtained.

This book is sold subject to the condition that it shall not by way of trade or otherwise, be lent, resold, hired out, or otherwise circulated without the publisher's prior consent in any form of binding or cover other than that in which it is published and without a similar condition including this condition being imposed on the subsequent purchaser.

Printed by BPUK

Playdead Press
www.playdeadpress.com

Contents

13
A Friend Request by Kate Collins

20
Father's Footsteps by Mary Cooper

32
Web Pal by Billy Cowan

40
A Change for the Better by Anne Neville

45
It Should Have Been Me by Billy Cowan

52
Cheers by Ged McKenna

M6 Theatre Company

Since its formation in 1977 as a pioneering TIE and community based Theatre Company, M6 has evolved into a renowned national and international touring Theatre Company, specialising in creating imaginative and relevant theatre with and for young audiences.

> *"Experts in producing theatre for young people"*
> **Manchester Evening News**

The Company has produced an extraordinarily varied and wide-ranging body of original work, which has extended the boundaries of theatre for young audiences; ground breaking bi-lingual performances, captivating multi-sensory theatre for the very young, contemporary monologues for teenage audiences and powerful productions for specific groups such as prisoners, their families and young people at risk.

M6's dynamic, original work is widely known for its strong emotional resonance and accessibility, setting the highest standards for artistic quality and making a unique artistic and educational contribution to the lives of thousands of young people from many different backgrounds.

From M6's Studio Theatre base in Rochdale, the Company's professional productions tour to over 16,000 children, young people and families each year at local, regional and national arts venues, nurseries, schools, community settings and international festivals; always balancing high profile opportunities with M6's strong commitment to reaching disadvantaged communities.

> *"The excellent M6"*
> **Lyn Gardner, The Guardian**

Recent work for young audiences and families has included:

Grandpa's Railway (5+)
Featuring a working model railway, live music and two very playful characters, Grandpa's Railway is a story about dealing with change. In the miniature world of his model railway everything is under Grandpa's control, but the real world throws up some difficult challenges for him. Through Grandma's optimism and encouragement he comes to realise that changing tracks can open up a whole new world. After a successful pilot tour of primary schools and community settings in Rochdale Borough, Grandpa's Railway embarked on a National tour which included a two week residency at The Unicorn, London.

Mavis Sparkle (4+)
Mixing illusion, science, music and animation, Mavis Sparkle is an ordinary character with an extraordinary dream, telling an inspiring story that is full of new discoveries and challenges pre-conceived ideas of who and what we are. The pilot tour to Rochdale primary schools and community settings was followed by a sell out national tour including performances at Oldham Linking primary schools and theatre venues in England, Scotland and Wales. This

was followed by a Christmas residency at Manchester's Royal Exchange Theatre.

Speech Bubbles
In partnership with London Bubble and working alongside Oldham Theatre workshop and Peoplescape Theatre, M6 delivered the innovative Speech Bubbles programme in Greater Manchester. The initiative supports the social and personal well-being of Key Stage 1 children through a specially designed programme of weekly drama workshop sessions. This evidence-based intervention helps the children by developing their speaking, listening and attention skills.

Act Now!
M6 Participatory Programme

The Act Now! programme is a Big Lottery, Reaching Communities funded project. It includes three regular youth theatre groups for ages 8-11, 12-14 and 15-18. It also includes Outreach projects, in partnership with local community and youth groups, schools, and various youth service providers such as Barnardo's and Shelter.

The programme also gives opportunities to participants to become young leaders by being part of the Act Now! panel. The panel is involved in project planning, evaluation and act as ambassadors for M6.

The Act Now! programme gives young people the chance to:

- Create and perform theatre
- Work with professional theatre makers
- Learn other skills such as dance, film, comedy and creative writing
- Gain confidence
- Make new friends
- Experiment, experience and explore
- Engage with, and feel proud of, their community
- Work with other young people from different cultural and social backgrounds

In September 2013, the Act Now! team launched a competition to find a new monologue to add to this collection. Using 'Act Now!' as a theme, writers under the age of 26 were asked to create an 8-10 minute monologue which was relevant to teenagers. After a panel of industry professionals decided on the short list, young people from M6 Youth Theatre were invited to share their views on the shortlisted monologues through a creative workshop. There were many fantastic entries which were of a high standard and 'A Friend Request' by Kate Collins was chosen as the winner. The team were very impressed by Kate's writing and the young people felt a connection with the subject matter of her monologue – the power of the online world. In 2014, Kate's monologue will be performed at the launch of the Act Now! Celebrate Youth Arts Festival, Oldham Bookmark Festival and Wigan Library Festival.

If you want to find out more about M6 Theatre Company and the Act Now! programme, please visit:

www.m6theatre.co.uk

M6's Contemporary Monologues

Alongside full-length productions, M6 has also developed a series of contemporary monologues (8-10 mins in length) written by a range of writers age 16-60 which can tour individually or as a collection. M6's first 6 monologues came from a competition mounted by the company in association with North West Playwrights in 2001. From 73 entries, 6 scripts were selected by young people for production. These toured as 'Double 6'. Since then M6 have held further competitions and commissioned many new monologues exploring specific issues.

This strand of work enables the Company to perform powerful contemporary stories in the classroom or theatre setting, providing young audiences with intimate, emotionally charged performances, which promote meaningful and important peer conversations.

Some of the touchstones M6 have developed for this work are:
- Dramatic monologues need to be just that; dramatic. They should not be prose enacted.
- We are meeting a character under pressure who, in this heightened state, is compelled to speak. They might be angry, sad, triumphant, desperate, apologetic, defensive, tempted or torn. Whatever the dominant emotion, something important is at stake. For example, in Weighed Down the character must make a decision about whether to accept her

father's invitation to spend Christmas with him and his new family in Florida. This could risk her relationship with her mother, her sense of identity – and possibly her health. Would the visit throw her back into self-destructive patterns or would it help her heal and move on? We are with her as she examines the dilemma in the light of her recent history.

- In each of the monologues we need to sympathise with, but not necessarily approve of the character.
- The character is on a journey, a journey in which a choice must be made or examined, a secret revealed or an uncomfortable decision justified. Whatever it is, it's a journey in which something happens. As with any play, the writer is showing the action not telling it. And as with any play, the writer should know precisely who the character is, where they are, what they want and why it's important. They should also know who the character is talking to; the audience as an audience, themselves, the new girl at school, a housing official, a best friend...
- In the short form monologues of M6 the action reaches a crisis but is not resolved.
- The audience engage with the character as a peer and become involved and moved by their predicament. This level of personal investment avoids the superficial and predicable responses that young people often fall back on in workshops.

Dot Wood (M6 Strategic Director) Mary Cooper (Writer)

"Excellent – they were completely captivated by both powerful scripts and performances"
Prestwich Arts College

"Spellbound – throughout the performance and at the end of the session, our students asked mature and relevant questions"
Woodhey High School

"All the monologues were equally effective. They held the audience captive because of their dramatic presentation"
Elton High School

"Our students had a fantastic experience. It benefited all of our students, it gave the opportunity to think and discuss"
Towneley High School

"The pupils enjoyed the range of issues presented and were receptive to the creative ways employed to present such ideas"
Falinge Park High School

A Friend Request
Kate Collins

JOSHUA is sitting cross legged on his bed. He looks about 16, fairly average, but something about him is slightly off. He wears simple black jeans, and a black hoodie with the hood pulled up. He looks almost ill and is sat in darkness. He opens his laptop or tablet and turns it on so that his face is illuminated by the light of the screen. He seems to be scrolling down, looking through profiles maybe. We hear a bleep as if someone has just entered a chatroom or signed on. He breaks into a smile and laughs quietly to himself.

Hello? Thank God you found me. I was beginning to get lonely - people do tend to get lost round here, so I reckon that must mean you're pretty smart, what with passwords and everything. It's good that you're smart. A lot of people seem to have missed that particular bus, don't you think? It's like one morning the whole world woke up dumb, and the minority that didn't were left around to babysit them. It's a funny old time, wouldn't you agree? Look, I know you don't know me - we've only just met, but I think you're smart enough to know what I'm doing here. I'd like to let you in on a secret.

There's never been a better time to be alive. It's like the age of now. Somebody gets shot halfway across the world and you'll find out about it within two minutes of it happening. Everything instant. Everything immediate. Patience isn't a virtue - information is, and information is everywhere. You could have them pissing themselves in 140 characters or less. It's simple. It so simple, it's beautiful.

You don't think I'm serious do you? You do know that the whole of the internet isn't just funny cat videos and cheap porn, right? There's so much more to it. There are things that nobody knows about. With the click of a button you could bring down a company, a government, a country. You could even get into a bank. A bank's operating system. Think of the havoc that would cause. *(Pause)*. You could do everything and anything. And you could do it from your laptop, your smartphone, your tablet computer. If you wanted to, you could sit in your bedroom wearing nothing but a onesie, stuffing your face with pizza, and single-handedly destroy a politician's reputation with just a dirty bit of trolling and a little help from me.

They keep saying that young people are the future. That we'll pave the way for generations to come. We're like their plan B: 'Whoops, we broke the ozone layer. Oh well it doesn't matter because the future generation will just patch it back together.' 'Economic crisis? I'll just file that under *see later*.' 'This poverty malarkey is dragging on a bit, isn't it? I'm sure it'll be fine in a couple of years.' We're cleaning up after them. We're the bloody maid-service! Now that's hardly fair, is it? But they're right you know - young people are the future. But you can bring the future to now. If you wanted to. You can get your voice heard. Social media was built by our generation, for our generation, and I don't know about you, but I wouldn't just sit around using it to 'like' posts about so-and-so's favourite band or stalk your best friend's older sister.

And even if -

His mobile rings. He pauses, looks at the number, looks frustrated and answers it sharply.

What? I mean, yeah, hi. Can you call me back I'm just... No... Fine... No, cos A equals B squared, plus C squared, minus A squared, *over* 2 BC... No, *over* 2 BC. Look, it's trigonometry, it's not bloody rocket science, just... Yes... Yes, then you do the inverse function. There you go. It's not like Miss Walsh is going to mark it anyway the stupid cow... Yeah... *(He laughs).* Fine, I'll help you with it tomorrow. I'm in the middle of something... Piss off! It's none of your business ... Yeah... Bye...

Hello? Hello? Are you still listening? Have you logged off? Oh, for f-

Oh, hi. I thought I'd lost you for a second there.

Look, I know it sounds odd, but they don't know you like I do. I understand. And I know how it feels. To be left out. It's not nice, is it? Everyone's always trying to stop me from getting what I want too. There's always a firewall, or software, or some bloody tech support waiting to stamp me out. Waiting to ruin the fun. Restrictions and limitations and rules - let them speak freely, but not too freely, right?

What I'm saying is if you act now - whilst you're young and smart, not sucked into their machine - you could sort it all out. Put the world to rights. Power to the people and all that. We could even be mates. That sounds good, don't you think?

It would be easy too. You wouldn't have to do much at all. You'd just have to give me a leg up - like friends do - and then sit back whilst I get to work. You'd do that for me, wouldn't you? You'd be blameless. It would be easy too. You'd do that for me, wouldn't you? And if anything bad were to happen, which it won't, I promise to keep you safe. I promise it'll be like you were never involved. And, at the end of the day, it's just a bit of fun really, isn't it? It's only online. It's not like you're killing anyone.

I wouldn't lie to you about this. I've got nothing to lose. But them - well, they lie all the time. It's in their nature. And you can't blame them, it's learned behaviour. See, smart people like you, you're clever enough to think for yourself. But the stupid people? All meandering along talking about the weather and school and the goddamn X-Factor - they need lies. Doesn't it make you sick? They're off idolising every car crash of a celebrity, every wannabe auto-tuned Barbie, but why not the real heroes? Dark Dante, SOLO, Edward Snowden - Masters of Deception! For the idiots out there, everything's always fine. There's always a solution 'in progress.' 'In progress'. What about now? Maybe we need a little re-shuffle. You have the power, Edward! *You!* You have connections, so help the cause!

I mean think. Really *think*. You'd be a hero. There's a whole lot to gain in this - not that it's about making money - well, not all of it anyway, but the honour of it. The grandeur. One step ahead of the times. The new Kevin Mitnick. They'll be printing your face on t-shirts. You'll be a regular Che Guevara.

So what do you think? Hello? Are... Are you still there? Hello?

What? You still don't believe me? I'm disappointed, I really am. Edward. I thought you knew what you were doing. I thought you were clever like me. But you're not, are you? Little rich kid. Just like your dad, eh? Just the son of a banker who'll never have to work a day in his life. Little posh boy. You, sat there, gormlessly staring into your computer screen, brain slowly rotting away, and you heard me. But you didn't listen, Edward. You didn't listen. I thought you were going to help me out. I thought you were going to be a good friend. I thought you were clever. But you're not.

Edward. Edward King. KingoftheWorld94. Password, Trojan11. Little sister, Elsie. First pet, Gizmo. Mother's maiden name, Parry. Edward. Edward King. I know where you live. I thought you were CLEVER. Clever. Edward. Clever Edward. Clever Eddie.

Sorry. I don't know what came over me. I just got a bit worried you were going to bottle out on me, Ed. You're not though, are you?

I didn't think so. Edward, the things we could do would blow your mind, they really would. I just need a hand. Just a little help, that's all I want. I'd do it myself, but, well, I'm more of a piggy-backer than a leader. You're the hero here, Ed. You're Champion of the World!

So, what do you say? I don't mean to rush you, Eddie, it's just I'm kind of here on a temporary basis. I can only hang around so long before things start to get a little complicated. All you have to do is give me the little thing that I need.

Just download me.

Let me in.

Okay? Okay?

END

Kate Collins

Kate is currently studying for her GCSEs, and hopes to do A-Levels and then go on to University (as it has been brought to her attention that 'superhero' isn't a valid profession.) Kate loves going to the theatre, and is currently participating in a Young Writers' course as a member of the Royal Exchange Theatre's Young Company in Manchester. This course has given Kate an opportunity to stretch her writing muscle and talk to people who write for a living.

In Kate's spare time, she likes to bake (with mixed results), listen to music and go for walks around her exotic homeland of the Wirral.

Kate is thrilled to have won the Act Now! monologue writing competition.

FATHER'S FOOTSTEPS
Mary Cooper

Nathan enters the room energetically. He is eighteen, well-built, young looking and, though he's doing his best to seem relaxed, he's twitchy, with lots of nervous energy. He's dressed in a suit with a white shirt and trainers. Despite his efforts to look smart, he looks uncomfortable; his jacket's too tight, his shirt collar is too big. He has a tie in his pocket, a mobile phone and a watch. He is carrying a small backpack containing clothes and a smart pair of shoes. We are in the side room of a crown court. Nathan has come in for sentencing, having pleaded guilty to GBH involving wounding. He will find out today whether he is going to prison or whether he'll receive a community sentence. There is a chair and a small table in the room. On the table there is a brown A4 envelope which contains Nathan's pre-sentence report.

NATHAN: Morning, morning. How do I look? Scrub up pretty good, don't I? Better than you. Look at you! Look like you've been sleeping in that suit! Should've got yourself a new one. You solicitors are paid enough. You got to look smart. It's my future on the line here. What's that? Toothpaste on your tie? Only joking.

He clocks the envelope, picks it up, clocks what it is.

Sentencing report, yeah?

Looks as if he's about to open it but instead taps it on the table a couple of times.

Know what it'll say, 'Mr Bateman this, Mr Bateman that… serious offence, previous convictions…' But I reckon if we can both, you know, say the right things an all, make the right impression, I won't… Well, it might not be so bad. Right?

He looks down at the envelope and puts it back on the table. Then with decision Nathan takes a tie from his pocket and begins to put it on while talking.

I know it's serious an all that. And the prosecution'll go on about Mossy still getting over it, but I pleaded guilty, didn't I. He makes out it's worse than it is, so's he can get compensation, so's he can get more money from Social.

I saw him out having a good time the other week.

Didn't want to know me. I had to go to another club. An I'd paid my entry, an all.

This whole thing'd never've happened if it hadn't been for that little prick asking me for I.D. I was three days off my eighteenth birthday, I'd just been served six pints of lager in the last place and then says he's not going to serve me. It should've been him, not Mossy.

But Mossy shouldn't've tried to stop me. He knows what I'm like.

He knows I just lose it, he knows I flip. He shouldn't have tried to get me outside. If he hadn't've, I'd never've gone for him. It would've been that little twat behind the bar.

How's that look? *(His tie.)* Good. Yeah.

The usher said we'd got about five minutes or so before we're called.

He takes some very shiny shoes out of his bag.

Didn't want them getting muddy on the way here.

He takes off his trainers and puts shoes on, while he's talking.

It'll be like last time, yeah? Prosecution'll go on about my previous and how I should be locked up for life (*He laughs nervously*) and then we'll get a chance to tell them; mitigating circumstances.

'Cause the offence was six months ago, more now, and since then everything's changed. I've calmed right down. Since Jayden was born. Before I was a… Dad, I didn't think about anyone else but myself, but now there's someone else to consider, someone to make a success of my life for. So they'd better not send me down.

I'm round at Becca's, looking after him whenever I can. I'm not out like I used to be.

You can tell court I've stopped drinking. You can tell court I'm going to college. 'Cause although I never got my GCSEs or anything, it wasn't cause I was thick. I wasn't. In fact I was very, very, very good at maths. I could just do it. At primary school I was in all the top groups, always was. Even though we kept moving schools. But when I went to high school, I was too busy taking motors and rallying through the woods to bother passing exams. If I'd've attended I could've got somewhere; gone to university even. 'Cause it always came easy.

What I'm going to do now is one of them short courses; plumbing, electrics. I'll earn good money and I'll be able to get nice things for the little 'un. I'm not going to go labouring; getting knackered out for peanuts.

He puts his hand in his pocket and takes out his watch.

Nobody I know wears a watch. But you do, don't you. I've noticed all you lot do. 'Cause a watch makes you look business-like. Like you've got somewhere to go. 'Time's money and all that.'

He puts on the watch.

I've started wearing one. 'Cause Becca, she's not right good at keeping him to his routines. Don't get me wrong, she's a good Mum and all that. But sometimes I'll go round flat and she won't have cleaned up and got him to bed and it'll be past seven. I have to tell her.

Like the other night, he hadn't got clean sheets and I made her go round to my mum's for some. There was milk spilled on his cot. She said it didn't matter. I told her. I'm not having my son sleeping in smelly sheets, no way. Not even for one night. My son's got to be looked after properly.

Slight pause.

She's got to be told.

He checks himself over, takes out his mobile.

Did I show you his picture?

He finds baby picture on his mobile and shows it to the audience.

Brilliant, in he? Everyone says he looks just like me. Poor sod.

He's finished 'dressing up' now but he's still hanging on to his mobile. He looks down at the envelope again, then back to his mobile. Slight pause.

I was watching telly at my Mum's when Becca's Mum rang. I was frozen, terrified. I just sat and watched the end of Who Wants To Be A Millionaire. 'Til my Mum shoved me into a taxi and sent me to the hospital. I hung about outside, looking at all these people going in with massive bunches of flowers – I didn't even have money for a cup of coffee. All I had in my pocket was a packet of Polos. When I got to labour ward, it was locked. I just couldn't ring bell. Then this midwife with a right stern face came up behind me and said, 'Who're here to see?' and she marched me straight in.

Becca was doing amazing but, she was in pain, you know. And midwife said to me, 'Comfort your girlfriend, Nathan.' I didn't know what to do, so I said, 'Do you want a Polo, Becs?' And she laughed, even though she was in pain, you know, and midwife laughed and I thought, 'It's going to be all right.' And half an hour later, he was born. And since then...

Pause. He puts his mobile away and looks down at the envelope.

I've seen him every day since he was born.

He picks up the envelope. He hesitates before opening it. He takes the report out of the envelope and glances at the front page.

Least they got my name and address right. Last time they'd got me down as Batman!

You know who wrote it, don't you? That creepy Jonathon from the Y.O.T. Him who was supervising my last order, the one who breached me 'cause I missed my appointments.

He turns to the next page, scans it.

Yeah, listen.

'Mr Bateman's response to his last period of supervision was less than satisfactory and following a third missed appointment... blah, blah, blah, blah, blah.'

(A decision to return him to court was made, only days before the current offence was committed.)

I'll tell you why I missed those appointments; 'cause he kept on giving me stupid things to do and asking me stupid questions.

Look, here.

'Mr Bateman describes a violent childhood where his father was physically abusive to him and his mother'.

He kept on about my Dad. He had me doing this spider thing, where you rate yourself on all sorts of stuff and I said, you know, my family relationships were, ten out of ten, sort of thing, but he wouldn't leave it alone. He made me write down a list of all my important relationships then he said, 'What about your Dad?' And I said, 'What about my dad? But he wouldn't leave it. He really wound me up.

He said, 'Well, I can see why you're angry with him.' I said,'
I'm not effing angry with him. I'm angry with you.' He was
lucky I didn't twat him.

That's why I missed the appointments, that's why I didn't
go back.

Slight pause.

You know about my Dad, don't you? You know he's a lifer?

Slight pause.

I've been thinking a lot about him since I've had Jayden.

My Mum left him when I was five. I've hardly seen him
since. My auntie's rung a couple of times and said, you
know, 'Your Dad'd like to see you.' But I've always said no.

Before he was in the nick he'd sometimes send me envelopes
full of money. I never took it, even if we could've done with
it, 'cause if I had, I'd've been admitting he's my Dad,
accepting I'm his son.

I sent it back to my Auntie. After I'd spat on it.

'Cause, you know, there's only one thing I remember about
him, really remember. I don't know how old I was, must've
been right little. I was playing in our back garden, kitchen
door was open. Maybe I heard something or… anyway, I

looked through the door and there was my Mum crouched against the wall, with her hands over her face – and his big shape standing over her. The way he looked at me when he saw me watching. All hard-eyed, you know. Then his hands came round the door and closed it - so's I couldn't see no more.

It's going to be different for Jayden. 'Cause I'm not like my Dad.

I'm not a bit like my Dad. Jayden's going to have a proper father.

Pause. He flips over the page of the report.

It's such a load of bollocks.

'In my opinion, Mr Bateman is an intelligent but troubled young man. (*Scanning*)... lack of skills in conflict resolution... adverse peer influence... and his emotional immaturity.'

He is getting angry. He can see from the tone of the report what's coming.

Crap. He doesn't know a thing about me.

'It is essential that a range of work is carried out with Mr Bateman... blah, blah, blah, blah, blah... should also be involved in further programmes addressing thinking skills, victim empathy and, above all, anger management.'

Beginning to get angry now.

Tosser. He's such a tosser.

'Mr Bateman does present a risk of harm to the public as highlighted by his previous violent offences and dangerous driving. He is classified by probation as medium risk.'

Come on! Where's it say…?

Pause. He reads it and then reads it out.

'It is evident that the only realistic disposal will be a custodial sentence.'

Now he really flips. Pointing the finger at his solicitor.

That means they're going to lock me up, doesn't it. That's what they're saying? You knew that? You've read the report. Why didn't you just tell me when I walked in. Then I needn't have bothered with all this.

He yanks off his tie.

Fucking Jonathon! And you said I'd get a community sentence.

Wrapped between his two fists the tie becomes a weapon.

You did, didn't you? You said I stood a chance. This isn't giving me a chance, is it? Well, is it? What about Jayden? If I miss him walking, talking ... He might not even remember me. You'd better do your job. You better get me off this. You'd better... 'Cause if you don't ...

USHER VOICE OVER: Nathan Bateman to Court Room Two please.

NATHAN: I'll kill him. I'll kill that fucking smooth probation officer.

USHER VOICE OVER: Nathan Bateman to Court Room Two.

NATHAN: Do you understand me?

He picks up his bag and exits.

END

Mary Cooper
Mary Cooper has written more than 25 plays to commission for theatre companies throughout England and Wales. She also writes for radio and screen.

Nathan's Story, *Father's Footsteps*, was written for Action for Prisoners' Families, and forms one half of a monologue 'double' *Family Business*. Mary has also written *Homeward Bound* and *Missing Out* for APF. The DVDs of all three plays are available from the APF website.
http://www.prisonersfamilies.org.uk/

WEB PAL
Billy Cowan

Zoe, a fifteen year old girl, stands suspiciously in front of a book rack in a bookshop. She keeps looking back and forth between the manager, who's behind the counter, and out of the shop window. We hear the rain outside.

That cow of a manager keeps looking at me, but I don't care coz it's a good look-out spot here - behind the books. Why do they always put cookery books with travel books? I mean, when you travel you aren't gonna cook, are you? You're gonna eat out in little cafes by the beach or fancy restaurants in the city or something like that. You're not gonna stay in your room and cook. That would be daft, wouldn't it?

Anyway, it's not my job to tell her how to run her stupid bookshop. I'm just here coz I've got a great view of McDonalds across the road, which means I'll see him but he won't be able to see me. I just hope that cow doesn't ask me to leave first.

I'm browsing, okay! Isn't that allowed?! Isn't that what people do in a crappy bookshop?!

It's because I'm young. She thinks I'm gonna nick one of the books. As if I'd be interested in a bloody cookery book anyway. And I doubt I'll ever be in Morocco or the bloody

French Pyreneesie, or whatever they're called – so why would I nick one of her books?

God, she's still looking at me. Right, I'm gonna close my eyes and count to ten. If she's still looking at me when I open them, I'll leave.

She closes her eyes.

Cinderella dressed in yella went upstairs to kiss a fella. By mistake she kissed a snake, how many kisses did she make?

One, two, three, four, five, six, seven, eight, nine, ten.

She opens her eyes.

Good. She's gone. Probably gone to get the police - no, that's crazy. I'm just being paranoid now. She's probably gone out back to make a cup of tea. I wish she'd make me one. I'm dying here - standing about like a muppet.

She looks at her watch.

Ten past. Five more minutes and he'll be here – waiting for me across the road in front of McDonalds.

I wonder if he'll look as nice as his profile pic. I hope he's wearing the same striped jumper, the one he said he got from Topman. Blues and yellows really really suit him, you see. Chantelle thinks he's too old to wear that kind of jumper but what does she know. She's just jealous coz she's never met anyone special on Facebook. All she gets is boys her own age sending her videoclips of themselves waving pretend guns about or pulling their trackies down and showing their bits off. She's never had anyone like Tommy.

'But it's not right, Zoe. He's too old for you.'

Blah, blah, blah. So what if he is older. At least he listens to me and talks to me about things that matter, like feelings and stuff. Not like the boys at school who only talk about football or Xbox and never let you get a word in edgeways. Tommy is ... mature. Yeah, mature. And I like that. He tells me how beautiful I am. Said I was like Joan of Arc. How cool is that? I didn't even know who Joan of Arc was until he told me about her. He also sends me poems – poems that he's written specially for me. He posts them onto my Funwall surrounded by little hearts and emoticons.

You came crashing into my life
Like a falling star from the sky
I don't know why
But I know it's meant to be
Cos only I understand you
And only you understand me

Isn't that cool? The boys I know wouldn't do that. They're more likely to post you some sick clip of a kid getting run over by a lorry or an old man getting happy-slapped on a bus or something.

Tommy would never do that. He's too sensitive. Last week he sent me a videoclip of a beautiful sunset on the island of Antigua. He said that he'd take me there someday.

Chantelle said, 'He's only being nice to you coz he's a pervert and a paedo.'

She thinks he's gonna take me away and sell me as a sex slave like one of those girls from Poland she saw on Channel Four the other night. I know she's my best mate and all but she's wrong there because it wasn't Tommy's idea to meet up, it was mine. And it was my idea not to tell mum. He wanted me to, but when I told him she'd freak out, he said it was probably better that I didn't then. He said it was best not to upset her. If he was a paedo or a pervert he wouldn't have said to tell my mum, now would he? And anyway, I'm not thick. I've just turned fifteen and I know there's men who crawl the internet looking to pick up young boys or girls. That's why I'm waiting here, out of sight, to see him first before I make up my mind.

If he is a freak or a perv I'll be able to tell coz they all have something weird about their eyes. Just look at photos of killers on the news, or old pictures of Myra Hindley and Ian Brady, or even Hannibal Lecter in Silence of the Lambs. They all have this strange look like they're seeing straight through you or something. If his eyes look like that, I'll just wait here until he leaves and then I'll go home and remove him from my friends list. Simple as.

She suddenly ducks down.

Oh my God, he's there. That's him. Well, I think it's him. He looks older than his profile pic.

Grabbing a book to hide behind, she looks up again.

Yeah, that's definitely him. But he does look older. I wonder if he used an old photo. But why would he do that? Maybe he doesn't like the way he looks. Yeah, that's it. I bet he thinks he's not good looking or something which is crazy coz he's quite fit for an older bloke. I mean, he's no Harry Stiles but he is ... nice. I don't think Tommy realises how nice he is though because he's so under-confident, which is why he doesn't have many friends on Facebook. He's too shy, you see. He said he only picked up the courage to ask me to be his friend because when he saw my profile he couldn't believe how much we had in common. And it's true. He loves rollercoasters and so do I. He thinks The Saturdays are tacky and so do I. And his Grandad died when he was ten just like mine. When you've got so much in common, age shouldn't matter, should it?

Oh God, he's looking at his watch now. He probably thinks I'm not gonna turn up. I really should go over. I mean... I like him and just because he looks a bit older than his profile pic doesn't mean he's been trying to trick me. I should just go over, say hello and go into McDonalds with him just for half an hour. I've come this far I might as well, and nothing bad can happen to me in Maccy D's with loads of people around.

The only thing I'm worried about though is mum. What if she walked in and saw me chatting to an older man when I'm supposed to be at Chantelles? She'd go mental. She's so over-protective and worries about everything. She wouldn't understand that Tommy is just a friend. A... pal. Yeah, a web pal. She wouldn't believe he's a nice and kind man, and she'd be really upset that I'd lied to her. I don't want to do anything to upset or disappoint her, she's had enough to cope with recently, but I don't want to upset Tommy either. He's the only person I can really talk to nowadays and he understands me better than anyone else ever ever has. Look at him – waiting for me in the rain – he's lovely. Who else would wait patiently like that for me?

I'm gonna have to make a decision and quick. That bitch of a manager's come back. I can't stay in here all day and Tommy won't wait forever. Why's it so difficult? I'm fifteen now I should be able to make my own decisions.

I know, I'll count to ten and when I reach ten I'll decide.

She closes her eyes.

Cinder... one, two, three, four, five, six, seven... eight... nine...

A long pause as she struggles with the decision.

Ten.

She opens her eyes.

END

Billy Cowan

Billy is a lecturer in Creative Writing at Edge Hill University and has an MPhil(B) in Playwriting from Birmingham University. He is also an award-winning playwright having won two international playwriting competitions – the Writing Out Award for Best New Gay play organised by Finborough Theatre London (2003) for *Smilin' Through* and Warehouse Theatre's International Playwriting competition 2010 for Transitions. He is also joint Artistic Director of Truant Company which was set up in 2004 to produce gay specific work.

His plays have been performed all around the country and include: *Smilin' Through* (2005) which was nominated for Best New Play of the Year at the Manchester Evening News Theatre awards. It was produced by Contact and the Birmingham Rep and was re-staged in 2007 at London's former Drill Hall.

Billy's other works include *Daddy* (B'ham Rep 2004), *Heart Is A Lonely Hunter* (Truant and 24:7 Theatre Festival, 2004), *Stigmata* (The Drill Hall 2006), *Care Takers* (Truant 2009/10) and *The Right Ballerina* (Truant 2012) which is also published by Playdead Press. *Care Takers* was selected by The Library Theatre Manchester as one of the best studio plays of 2009 and was remounted at their Re:Play festival in 2010.Billy is also an applied theatre practitioner and has worked extensively for the Oldham Coliseum and M6 Theatre Company, as well as working freelance for many other theatre companies in the North West.

A CHANGE FOR THE BETTER
Anne Neville

The withdrawal room in a mainstream primary school. A child's chair and an adult's chair stand beside a small table. On the wall behind are an eyesight testing chart and an environmental poster. The room is used for children to be seen by visiting medical and educational professionals. The door of the room shuts and adult footsteps are heard walking away. Ten year old Ian, dressed smartly in school uniform and carrying a plastic box, walks slowly towards the table. He has a language and learning disability. He is repeating instructions to himself.

IAN: Here's the room, Ian. In you go. Okay? Sit down on the small chair and wait.

He sits on the small chair.

IAN: Someone's coming in to see you. Sit and wait. Won't be long.

He puts his hands on the box.

IAN: Keep your lego in the box. Okay?

Ian sits straight and tense on the chair. He looks towards the door and listens for footsteps. hearing nothing, he opens the box of lego.

IAN: Legoland.

From the box he takes some lego pieces and a small lego figure which he holds in his hand.

IAN: Legoland.

He smiles at the audience.

IAN: Remember, special Legoland Plan. Old School Legoland Plan. When you follow the numbers because the design.

He starts carefully arranging the lego pieces on the table in front of him.

IAN: Remember Jason say, 'Magic numbers, Ian. These numbers are like magic.' Working together Knight's Castle Lego Duplo. Not home time yet. Time to choose activity. And Jason say, 'Mrs Connolly, me and Ian choose Knight's Castle.' 'Not again,' Robbie say. 'Jason and Ian choose Knight's Castle again!' And Mrs Connolly very helpful. 'That's fine, boys. Follow Knight's Castle numbers carefully. It's looking good.' Looking good and if when finished not break in pieces. Up on safe shelf and thank you Mrs Connolly. Bring down again when time to choose. Come on, Jason! Let's choose same again!

Sound of footsteps approaching along the corridor. Ian hastily separates the lego pieces and puts them back in the box.

IAN: Pack it away, Ian.

Steps continue on past the door. His hands relax and he puts the box of lego down on the table.

IAN: Pack it all away. Well done. Remember need to pack it away old school. Mum and Dad go important meeting and man at meeting say, 'Change for the Better. Children go

Change for the Better School.' Pack away old school. Everybody help and working hard. 'Good work, Jason and Ian, that looks really neat and tidy.' And then big closing down party. Dance to music and this is a really special cake. 'Mrs Connolly, why you not come Change for the Better School?' Pack it away. Remember.

He puts the box of lego into his pocket.

IAN: And then time Change for the Better and put on new school uniform, very smart, and new teacher say, 'Children, this is Ian. You sit here Ian.' Sit and listen. And listen very hard and try very hard. Listen hard and they say hard words and Sir say, 'Don't call out to answer. Put your hand up.'

Ian puts his hand up.

IAN: 'Yes, Ian?' And say, 'I think. I think . . .' 'Yes, Ian?' And mix up words. And can't say. Children staring. All children staring. 'Alright, Ian'. And sit quiet. And they say lots more of words and very lots more. And very by myself. Sit quiet.

Ian sits in silence.

IAN: And Mum I don't know where is Jason. Jason was lost. And this is a TV News item. Because whether a minibus was involved and young boy dead at scene. Name Jason. 'No, no, Ian love, it's not your Jason. That's down in Birmingham, okay? That's a different Jason'. But I don't know where is.

Ian takes the lego out of his pocket again and plays with it.

IAN: When is playtime can put my lego on the wall. Can take out of the box and can make something. And Mrs Porter will kindly help you and saying, 'Ian, let me mind your lego and you come and be friends with the children.' And Mrs Porter take lego.

Ian sweeps the lego to one side.

IAN: And we do walk all the way over to the children and I do say, 'Sorry to bother you.' And children laughing saying, 'Sorry to bother you! Sorry to bother you!' Joke not funny. And talking, talking, talking. Not funny. Not funny. And shout at children. And shout, 'Where is my lego?' And Mrs Rogers come fast all the way over. And Mrs Rogers speak Mrs Porter and saying, 'Let him have his lego, Liz. These children are in a world of their own.'

Ian sweeps the lego across the table back in front of him.

IAN: I got an idea. Good idea where is Jason. Jason is gone world of their own.

END

Anne Neville

Nev studied Drama and Literature at Bristol University and did graduate work in Leeds and the USA.

With a young family she changed course to qualify as a therapist and for 35 years worked closely with children with language and communication disorders. On account of this job and because two of her grandchildren have communication disorders, she spent a lot of time up close with Special Education. Language assessment and therapy often involved recording, transcribing and analysing conversations with the children. In these scripts there was a poetry and drama which checklists and statistics disregarded.

Having done occasional writing for the stage as a student and for political street theatre, Nev is lucky in retirement to be living in Greater Manchester with its diverse grass roots opportunities for script writers. As the writing element of Disordered Speech she has had work performed at the 24:7 Theatre Festival and at various local venues, currently at Smiths Theatre Restaurant. Working with M6 and its audience was of special importance to her.

It Should Have Been Me
Billy Cowan

An empty classroom. Sophie, a 15 year old schoolgirl, enters quickly closing the door behind her. She's been crying and wipes her eyes. She waits a few moments and then pops her head out the door to see if anyone is about. She comes back into the classroom and runs over to the whiteboard. She grabs a marker and starts to write in big letters JOSH DUNNE IS... She hesitates. Her mobile phone rings. She looks at who's calling, then answers.

What? *(Pause)* I'm down the park with Abs. Where are you? *(Pause)* Oh. *(Pause)* Yeah, I'm chilled. *(Pause)* I am, alright! *(Pause)* Nah. *(Pause)* I just don't! Abs and me are going to town. *(Pause)* Yeah, whatever.

She ends the call, upset.

'Do you wanna come up to Marks?' No, I don't shitting wanna come up to posh boy Marks! What a great laugh that would be, not! Me and them. Me sitting in a corner like a pot plant watching them do whatever, dance to Kylie or whatever they do. I don't think so.

She becomes upset again.

I thought it was going to be me. Me. What an idiot, a stupid cow. How could I be so blind?

'Sophie, I've got something big to tell you,' he said. 'Something really important.'

I thought this is it, at last. The moment I've been waiting for and then when he said it... I just stopped breathing. Literally stopped breathing. It felt like someone had put a really tight elastic band around my throat. I couldn't speak. I could feel the tears well up. He asked if I was alright about it. I lied and nodded, then I just ran away.

Pause.

I hate him. I really hate him.

She gets upset again.

It should have been me. Why wasn't it me? We've seen each other every day for the past six months. I thought he felt like I felt. He did, I'm sure of it. You can't mistake those things. I mean he never kissed me but he was always hugging me, telling me how great I was, how smart I was. He'd always sit on me on the swings in the park, wrapping his legs around me as we talked and talked and swung back and forth for hours. You don't do that unless you really like someone, do you?

I thought he was my soul mate coz right from the start we got on really well. It was at Ab's sixteenth, down at The Legion. Her dad had hired out the hall and there were tables with everyone's names on them. She'd put Josh beside me coz she thought we'd get on. She laughed and said he was a bit of a freak, like me. Two Emo's who could sit in a room together, she said, and never see the light of day while reading crap stupid books about vampires or whatever. Abs is mouthy and sarcastic like that but she was right, we got on like a house on fire right from the moment he sat down and said how cool my black nail polish was. That's what I love about him, the way he always notices things about me, like if my hair has just been styled or I'm wearing a new top or summat. And he isn't afraid to tell me if he doesn't like it either. In fact, if he doesn't he goes back to the shop with me and helps me choose something else. And he's always right about it. Like about two weeks ago right I got this pink dress from Afflecks which had tiny little black skulls all over it. I thought it was kinda cool and ironic like in an Eighties retro goth kind a way but when he saw it he practically gagged, said it was horrible, said it was so not my colour, that it clashed with my skin which had too much yellow in it. He said it made me look like an iced bun or summat, which made us both laugh. But he was right of course. So he took me back and made me change it for a purple one which suited my skin colouring much better. Everyone said so. That's what I like about him, the way he cares how I look, the way he takes an interest. Other boys aren't like that. It's like you're invisible to them. They don't notice anything about you and they don't listen to you. All they do is talk about themselves, whereas Josh likes to be quiet sometimes and listen to me. Why can't all boys be like that?

Her mobile beeps with an incoming message. She picks it up and then puts it back into her blazer without reading it.

That'll be him. But I'm not gonna look at it. He'll know I'm upset. How could I not be? And he'll be worried... but I don't care. When he comes into school tomorrow he'll have a lot more to worry about after I've spilled the beans.

She looks at the whiteboard and grabs the marker.

I know it's kinda childish and cruel, but... I hate him and he deserves it. He should have told me sooner before I fell in... I mean, he must have been blind not to see. Unless he knew and just didn't care. Maybe it made him feel good to have a girl like me follow him around like a big soft stupid puppy dog. Maybe he was using me to hide the fact he was... yeah, I bet that was it. Well, I'll show him not to mess with me.

She goes to the whiteboard and begins to write GAY but hesitates after the letter G.

Josh wouldn't do that though. Especially to me. I know he wouldn't. There's not a cruel bone in his body except when he's bitching about the saddo's who go on Britain's Got Talent. He wouldn't treat me bad like that. I mean, he's so kind and thoughtful. He helps me do the shopping for mum when she's too depressed to do it. He doesn't even mind it when I have to take little Leah out with us when mum needs some head space. He even wheels the buggy for me. He's done so many nice things for me since we started hanging out like paying for the cinemas when I haven't got any money or giving me free subs when I come into see him in Subways on Saturdays. When it was my fifteenth he took me out to Pizza Express, yeah Pizza Express not Pizza Hut, and I didn't have to pay a penny. And we had three courses. Three courses. And that wasn't the end of it. When we got back home he said he wanted us to climb the tree in my back garden like Edward and Bella from Twilight. I thought he was well mad but we did it anyway and when we got up he showed me a little box which was tied to one of the branches. He told me to open it. Inside was a silver charm bracelet with a big glass heart on it, just like Bella Swans. He said he wanted to do something special for me as it's not everyday you turn fifteen. And he wanted me to remember it. There's no way you'd do those type of things for someone if you were just using them. (*Pause*) Maybe I should look at his message.

She takes the mobile out and reads the message.

He says please don't be upset. You're still my best mate and always will be even if you can't accept it. I'm here to talk whenever you're ready. Big kiss.

She gets upset again.

It should have been me. What's wrong with me? I know I'm not Cheryl Cole but I'm not bad looking. And I'm funny. I make Josh laugh all the time. We spend every minute together and everyone in the whole school thinks we're going out anyway because they can see how close we are. Abs, Megan, Ellie and Danielle think we were made for each other. Now everyone will know we aren't. Now everyone will know he's been making a fool outta me. Everyone will laugh, no doubt. Mum'll say I told you so coz she's always telling me how shit men are and that I should stay well clear of them. When I used to shout back that Josh was different she'd laugh and say 'we'll see Soph, we'll see.' I hate it when she's right and I hate Josh for making me look pathetic.

She marches to the whiteboard and grabs the marker. Angrily she finishes the sentence:

JOSH DUNNE IS GAY – FACT! ASK MARK ROBERTS

She stands back and looks at it.

When all his classmates walk in tomorrow and see this, he'll be sorry. Deserves him right.

She marches towards the door, then stops.

What if they hurt him though? What if they start to bully him really badly? He could end up in hospital or worse? There's some real hard lads in this school like Gonzo Riley and Pete Wallace. They hate gay boys and if they found out... God, it's not worth thinking about. I'd never forgive myself if something bad happened to Josh. I mean, he's my best friend... my soul mate. (*Pause*) I can't do this.

She goes back to the whiteboard. She lifts the duster and rubs off some of the words. She then hesitates.

But… it should have been me. He should've loved me.

She puts the duster down and lifts the marker. She looks at it not knowing what to do.

END

CHEERS
Ged McKenna

An armchair. A coffee table on which is a copy of 'TV Quick,' an ashtray full of fags and a cuddly toy belonging to Shannon. Ben 14, enters carrying a mug of tea. He's talking quietly to his younger sister.

BEN: You go to sleep, Shannon. It's late... No, mummy's asleep. Court tomorrow. Now be a good girl. Night night.

He sits in the armchair and picks up the TV Quick. He flicks through it, then chucks it down.

BEN: I finally did it. You know the way things build up. Well, it's been building up like a spot you squeeze and squeeze for ages and ages and then it finally pops and all the gunge comes out all yellow and bloody and... that's mingin' that, isn't it? I think of things sometimes and I just say them. My Nanna says it's wiser to keep your own counsel; she talks like that, but I think if things need saying, then you should just say them. How are things gonna change if you don't?

He drinks.

BEN: And here we are now... It's not a bad place. It's a bit damp in the bathroom and people piss in the lift sometimes, but like Mum says. 'It's home.' She didn't want to go to the refuge again, cos she says people try and talk to you too much there, so we're here...

He moves to the window and looks out.

BEN: You can see right across the city. All the lights and that. Above all the cranes, and Argos and Next and B&Q. Above it all. I keep saying to our Shan, 'Look at all that, Shannon, the whole world in front of our window.' But she's well miserable. She misses my Dad... well, it's just tough. They'll bail him and then it'll just... Got to be cruel to be kind, innit?

He sits back down.

BEN: I hear my Mum crying an' all sometimes. At night. I said to her this morning,' 'Are you alright?' And she did that smile she does and said, 'Why wouldn't I be? Now come on, get your breakfast and do your fly up, Ben, you'll get arrested.' 'Runs in the family,' I said. Joking like. But that went down like a turd in a swimming pool.

He reads the telly paper again, the horoscopes.

BEN: Aries. There are important decisions to be made and only you can make them. Thanks pal.

He chucks the paper.

BEN: My dad's great mostly. You can have a real laugh with him. We've had season tickets for the match for as long as I can remember and he's brilliant at birthdays and Christmas and all that. He was dead funny... once. When I was about seven and you believe in Father Christmas and all that, even though you see loads of them around the shops and you say to your Mum, 'How many are there?' and she really tas~~

He takes another drink.

And you buy it, don't you? Anyway, this
Eve, my Mum had made us crackers and cheese when ~
come in, and we was dancin' to Duran Duran. *(He sings)*
Oh-oh, this is Planet Earth, We're goin' to Planet Earth.
Ba, ba, ba, Bah ba ba ba ba, This is Planet earth – cos they
both love them, Duran Duran, and I had my feet on hers
and we was boppin' about like mad people and he was
pretendin' to sing into the salty thing, strikin' poses, and my
Mum was laughin' so much she near pissed herself. It was
brilliant, and I got dead excited, you know, and she said,
'Come on Sweetheart, time for bed. You don't want to keep
Santa waitin', do you?' And I was torn, you know – I didn't
want to leave it cos we were havin' such a great time, but
Santa was comin'. So my Dad gave me a little taste of his
wine and said, 'There you go, that'll help you sleep.' This
was before our Shannon was born. And they put me to bed
and kissed me goodnight, but I was just like mega excited
cos Mum had said Santa was gonna bring me a mountain
bike if I was a good boy and I'd been well good, so I just
couldn't sleep... And I suppose it must've been about eleven
o'clock and I heard this creaking out on the landing and then
the door opened just a crack and the light made a stripe on
the curtain and I thought, Santa's here! And I pretended to
be asleep, only I could see out through the bottom of my
eyes, and the door opened. I could hear the telly downstairs,
and this big figure come in carrying the Christmas sack that

I always woke up to on Christmas mornings, and he banged his leg on the chest of drawers and he said really soft, 'Bollocks.' And then he put the sack down at the foot of the bed and leant down and kissed me on the head. Here.

He points to his forehead.

And I could smell the stuff on him. It was kind of a sweet and warm smell. Then he was gone. He closed the door really softly. I listened to him going downstairs, then I got my torch out and had a look in the sack and there was a bike helmet and I knew I'd got my bike, but I knew too that... it wasn't Father Christmas. It was Dad pissed up. Funny, eh?

He drinks.

My Mum loves him, I know that. Even though he hits her. She's said it's her fault before now, and she has moaned at him on occasions, but he shouldn't be lampin' her... I don't want us to go back again. He'll be all nice and sayin' sorry and buyin' us stuff, 'specially for Shannon and givin' her cuddles cos she loves that; he gets her head under his arm and pretends he can't find it... And tryin' to explain to me about losin' his temper and it not bein' him. But it is, isn't it? It is him... He says the Devil's in the drink, but he drinks it, doesn't he? He knows it's in there and he still drinks it...

Pause.

My Mum drinks. When we've gone to bed. She says it's only to help her sleep, but I don't know if it is. Why should she need help sleepin' when she's lookin' after us and workin' in that shop? Well, she can't work at the minute cos her arm's broke, but usually... 'I slipped,' she said, when the police came. But only after he hit her. That's not a proper accident slippin', that's bein' decked. He just... he just goes off like he's off his head, and then he cries about it after. It's not our fault he doesn't like his job... she used to answer back, but she doesn't even do that now and he says, 'Don't you fuckin' ignore me!' And bang – she's across the kitchen again.

He's upset now, but intent on containing it.

I look at her and she's just got scared in her eyes all the time... I suppose people'd say I'm a grass. That I've grassed my own dad up. My mate, Ahmed, he says his dad says what happens in a family should stay in a family. That's what makes it strong. But I think that's rubbish. It just puts a wall up and nobody can get out. I mean, I see my Mum bleedin' and him cryin' and her holdin' him and sayin', 'It's alright darlin'. And strokin' his head and I think that's not right! So I do somethin' about it. I all the Police and I say I'm a witness and I say I want him locked up till he sorts himself out. Proper. And he's shoutin' Leanne! Leanne! as they drag him out and she's cryin' and shoutin', 'You've hurt me! You've hurt me!' And our Shannon's just...

Pause.

I love him, you know. He's a laugh. My mates think he's awesome... And now everyone's unhappy and it's my fault... My mum says she's not gonna drop the charges this time, but it'll kill her if he goes to prison. But he might kill her if he doesn't... You should hear my Nanna, 'You made your bed, Leanne, you got to lie in it now.' That don't help, does it?

Pause.

I don't know what will...

END

Ged McKenna

Trained at Central School of Speech and Drama and continues to work as an actor. He has worked for The RNT, The Royal Court (London), The Traverse, The Bush, Shared Experience, Cheek by Jowl, The English Theatre, Frankfurt and many reps around the country as well as appearing on TV in a variety of drama's including *The Bill*, *Casualty*, *Holby City*, *Doctors*, *Coronation Street* etc. He has written several plays, some of which, like *The Farmer's Bride* which began life at The Stephen Joseph Theatre, Scarborough and toured extensively in 1997, have been produced. He was born in Liverpool and lives in Chester.